Time For Play

by Brooke Summers-Perry

For Chase, Link, and Scout.
For *all* the kids who are waking up their parents, teachers, and clergy.
To the nonviolent revolutionaries that dare to understand, know,
and love themselves enough to dare to understand, know
and love everyone else for who they are.
For the kids that keep asking the why questions.
For all those who accept that we are doing the best we can.
For all those daring enough to be who they are and love who they love.
For the everyday moments that make memories.
For all of us that want to find our way with integrity, respect, love,
equality, competence, community, connection, and contribution.

For each of us........equally.

In memory of my co-workers who passed into full unity years ago.
To Amy: the illustrations that were found in your desk have never left my heart.
To Diana: you lived your short life in such a way that your memory continues
to be a spiritual guide. Because of the two of you, my mind and heart were open
to the possibility of writing and illustrating a children's book.
Even if this book isn't seen outside our house, it has worked its magic here in
my heart and in the heart connection with our kids.

Copyright 2014 Brooke Summers-Perry
www.key2peace.com
All rights reserved. No part of this publication may be reproduced.

This book refers to parenting with Compassionate Communication, also known as *Nonviolent Communication (NVC)*, based on the work of Marshall Rosenberg, PhD..

Some basic principles of *NVC*:
We all have the same set of needs (values).
Every person's needs matter equally.
Our perception alone determines our sense of fulfillment of each need.
We use different strategies to get our needs met.
Conflict is a result of strategies clashing with other strategies.
Our feelings signal whether or not our needs are met.
We have a better chance of connecting with our own needs
and others' needs, when we differentiate our judging thoughts
from what we can objectively observe.

Resources:

cnvc.org - Books, CDs, webinars, and other *Nonviolent Communication (NVC)* resources based on the work of Marshall Rosenberg, PhD and others all over the world who are spreading the gift in this work.

Other *NVC* websites with great resources:
houstonnvc.org
baynvc.org
radicalcompassion.com

The author's website
key2peace.com, includes tools, practices, and reflections on the author's experience with compassionate communication (*NVC*) in parenting, partnering, and spirituality.

I wake up and see my favorite toy.
You say, "It's time to get ready, big boy."

I'm eating my breakfast,
I play with my food.
You say, "Don't make
a mess.
That's rude."

We get in the car. I'm strapped in my seat.
You turn on music.
I start kicking my feet.
You tell me to stop, be still, and sit quiet.

If I don't play soon I'm starting a RIOT!

We get to school. My friends are in class.
You ask for a kiss. I give you some sass.

The teacher asks me to sit in my spot. I am so mad. My face feels hot!

I sit and listen with all my might.
My body is restless.
I run out of sight.

I end up in the time out chair.
I'm so mad.
I sit and stare.

When time out is over,
it's outside for play.
"Finally", I say, "It's been half the day!"

The teacher is happy I turned things around.
It's easy after being on the playground!

After our lesson, it's time for a nap.
I am ready to go and fall asleep in a snap.

I wake and guess what? I'm ready to play!

You pick me up,
"We've got errands," you say.

We buy some food at the grocery store.
We go home for dinner. I want to play more.

We go to your friend's house, and I try to wait.
You talk so long that it gets really late.

I found a long object. I pretend it's a snake.
Who knew if I touched it it was going to break?
I am frustrated,
I'm mad,
and I'm sorry;
that's true.

I'm just wanting
something
more fun
to do!

Can we talk about new ways to play?
I think I need some all
through the
day.

In the morning I can give you time to say hi to your stuff.

Do you think 10 minutes will be enough?

We can listen to your favorite song on our way to school. You can dance, kick, and sing. Would that be cool?

"Can we play I spy in the parking lot before I go into school and sit in my spot?"

When you pick me up and tell me what we're going to do, will you ask me what I want to do too?

The author is a student of
Compassionate Communication (nvc).
Her three children, Chase, Link, and Scout
are her best teachers.

Her reflections and insights are available
at spiritualspark-asif.blogspot.com

Time For Play
copyright Brooke Summers-Perry 2014

Time For Play
copyright 2014
Brooke Summers-Perry

www.ingramcontent.com/pod-product-compliance
Lightning Source LLC
Chambersburg PA
CBHW042129040426
42450CB00002B/133